ALONE WITH HIM

Corey Broussard

Copyright © 2024 by Corey Broussard

All rights reserved. No part of this publication may be reproduced, stored or transmitted in any form or by any means, electronic, mechanical, photocopying, recording, scanning, or otherwise without written permission from the publisher. It is illegal to copy this book, post it to a website, or distribute it by any other means without permission.

Corey Broussard asserts the moral right to be identified as the author of this work.

Scripture quotations marked NLT are taken from the Holy Bible, New Living Translation, copyright © 1996, 2004, 2007, 2013 by Tyndale House Foundation. Used by permission of Tyndale House Publishers, Inc., Carol Stream, Illinois 60188. All rights reserved.

Scripture quotations marked KJV are from the King James Version of the Bible, which is public domain.

First edition

This book was professionally typeset by Great Books

Contents

Introduction   iv
1. Find Me O' God   1
2. Surrender   3
3. Perspective   5
4. Brutal Honesty   9
5. Intimacy   12
6. Sovereignty   15
7. Trust   16
8. It's All For Him   18
9. His Kingdom   20
10. Battling Uncertainty   22
11. Acknowledge   24
12. Change Your Mindset   27

Introduction

The purpose of this poetic devotional is to help you spend time alone with the God of all creation. I often hear the phrase, "More of Him is always the answer," and I have found this to be true. He is everything, and seeking Him in every situation brings growth and maturity through intimacy with the Master.

This devotional will share thoughts that God has revealed to me as I sought a deeper relationship with Him. Find a quiet space where you can be alone with Him and let God speak to you.

Each month will have a weekly focus:

- **Week 1 - Change Your Mind:** Focus on adjusting your mindset and thought processes. Meditate on the month's devotional and scripture while seeking God for greater understanding.

- **Week 2 - Change Your Behavior:** Put this new way of thinking into action. Pray for opportunities to practice your new mindset.

- **Week 3 - Change Your Life:** Focus on your "new normal."

Let your renewed mindset guide your daily actions. Remember, Rome wasn't built in a day, so take each step with confidence until this becomes your way of life.

- **Week 4 - Change a Life:** When you feel strong, pray for a divine connection with someone who will benefit from your new insights.

As you go through this devotional, believe that God wants a deeper connection with you. Trust that He can and will cultivate a relationship that thrives in storms, grows through battles, and increases in intimacy.

1

Find Me O' God

Father, You left the 99 to search for me.

You came to me in the midst of my mess, and who I had become was not what you had designed.

Call forth in me the seed You created.

Cover it, cultivate it, and feed it. Embrace it and breathe Your life over it.

Find me, O God, and cause me to rise up anew and become who it is that you've designed me to be.

Beauty of His Creation, spring forth in me.

Majestic words of my Master Creator, unfold me over until all that is left is what is revealed by the tender words You whisper into my very being.

Sovereign One, bring forth all You desire to see.

May Your Kingdom come in us as it is in Heaven.

Forgive me—for I have agreed with lesser things in an attempt to justify, in my small mind, the struggles I face.

I have accepted circumstances, adjusted my way of thinking, and my way of life to accommodate things that were never meant to be.

In all things, may Your will be done.

Grant me the grace and the strength to live out Heaven on Earth.

2

Surrender

"Commit thy way unto the Lord; trust also in Him; and He shall bring it to pass." Psalm 37:5

First and foremost, let me state that God is inherently good. He desires more than anything to heal you from the "god" you are currently using to numb the pain from a history you've been afraid to even talk about.

"The enemy of our soul cannot deceive a vessel who doesn't need an explanation from God." - Prophet Dyron Adams.

The enemy cannot win over a bride who doesn't require or ask God why they are going through a specific season of discomfort. When you surrender control to the King of all eternity, you trust in His goodness towards you above all else. From personal experience, you will know that no matter the outcome, your situation will work for your good.

We don't need an explanation from our King. We don't need an answer why. We don't even need to know when or how. We live with mystery—the "not knowing"—because we trust He is good, and we will see His goodness in the land of the living.

Give Him complete control of all things for one sole purpose: that you may know Him more!

3

Perspective

"Then the Lord God called to the man, 'Where are you?' He replied, 'I heard you walking in the garden, so I hid. I was afraid because I was naked.' Then the Lord God called to the man, 'Who told you that you were naked?'" Genesis 3:9-11 NLT

Before you were ever formed in your mother's womb, God spoke over you what He desired for your life. He declared your end from your beginning.

These statements may bring questions to mind...

"THIS!? This is how I am supposed to be?

"This is how I'm meant to live... this torment?

"This confusion and shame? THIS IS IT!?"

NOT-AT-ALL. Choices that were made, trauma beyond your control, and the coping mechanisms you embraced in an attempt to mask the pain—all these contribute to what your life looks like currently.

What I have been blessed to see and am continually unraveling has drastically shifted my way of thinking.

Allow me to dispel the lies of the enemy over your mind. Just because you are tempted with sin and those thoughts continually bombard your every waking moment does not mean you are that sin. Just because the temptation comes, does not mean that which the temptation is attempting to make you believe is true.

But if you can be honest, you believed it. You jumped in with your full weight and took part in all that sin had to offer. You rolled in the pigpen, and thus you believed that this is who you are.

By society's standards, what you have done determines your identity. Even the Church is quick to label someone according to their current actions, finding an innate need to identify someone by what they have done.

However, our Father views your identity through the lens of what He spoke over you before He formed you. Don't get me wrong, He most definitely sees your errors and your faults. Still He says:

> *"That is what they are doing, NOT who they are."*

Although you took full part in all of the actions tied to that identity, today He asks:

> *"Who told you that is who you are? Because I didn't."*

Who God says you are hasn't changed because of your actions. Your identity is tied to His Word over your life. You can trust His words over your life. So go forward, allowing yourself the honor of living a life in pursuit of Him. He is the answer, and He will cause you to become all you were designed to be as you spend time alone with Him.

Just as He spoke to Adam and Eve in the garden after they had eaten of the forbidden fruit, today He asks:

> *"Who told you—Who told you that is who you are?"*

Bring Mephiboseth to Me

How will I feed them if My people won't go?
How will I heal them if My people won't reach?
I sat with sinners, with the hated ones, because they needed Me.
They would appreciate the miracles I would do for them more than My own chosen ones.
Self-righteousness says, "I don't need a Savior, I am Abraham's seed. I keep the commandments perfectly and I follow the law, therefore I am good."
Today, self-righteousness has silenced the voice of the hurting and maimed ones.
Self-righteousness isn't comfortable with dirt and mess, so the hurting are ignored and shamed into silence.
You see, human nature is afraid of what it cannot understand.
The need for today is a place for the hurting to just sit and be open about what they are fighting.
A place where they can feel free to release what is hurting.
The King of Creation says, *"I give them a place at My table where their handicap is hidden by My provision and grace. Seated with Me, there is nothing that cannot be transformed into beauty."*

4

Brutal Honesty

"Then the word of the Lord came unto me, saying, 'Before I formed thee in the belly, I knew thee; and before thou camest forth out of the womb, I sanctified thee, and I ordained thee a prophet to the nations.' Then said I, 'Ah, Lord GOD, behold, I cannot speak, for I am a child.' But the Lord said unto me, 'Say not, I am a child: for thou shalt go to all that I shall send thee, and whatsoever I command thee thou shalt speak.'" Jeremiah 1:4-5

Give yourself permission to be completely honest with yourself and God about what you're experiencing and how you feel about it.

Many times, our struggles breed shame and self-hatred when we do not experience complete healing from traumatic events. When we don't experience total deliverance from what keeps us trapped in negative cycles, we tend to distance ourselves from our Father in shame because we feel we aren't good enough.

One thing you must learn in your pursuit of intimacy with Him is that temptation is separate from acting on that temptation. Just because you are tempted by sin does not mean you are of that sin.

Often, our past follows us, haunting our minds with thoughts and desires. The constant barrage of attacks can become overwhelming and weaken us if we don't understand how to combat it. We must separate the temptation from our actual identity.

Let me say it again: **just because you are tempted by it does not mean you are it.**

One thing God has graciously allowed me to see is how much of an honor it is to simply talk with Him about everything. I've allowed myself to be completely vulnerable and open with Him. Yes, even the dirty parts—the feelings, the thoughts, what I felt about them, what my reactions were at that moment. (Hey, it's not like He doesn't already know it all anyway.) I then stop and ask Him what He thinks about the whole situation. I ask Him how He wants me to view it and then attempt to train my mind to see it like Him from that moment forward.

His view is the only thing I want to see. His opinion is the only opinion I can afford to have.

- Pray daily for His mind over your life.
- Ask Him what He spoke over you before you were ever formed in your mother's womb.

That is your identity—Your Creator spoke it into existence. You will do all that He has declared that you should do, and you will go wherever He will send you.

Even Isaiah struggled with the feeling that he wasn't enough for the assignment God placed on his life. But God reassured him that his identity was far more than the minimal view he had of himself. He then took the time to build confidence in Isaiah by confirming that He would give him the words he would need to speak in every situation He would send him into.

Rest assured, He is aware of where you came from and all that you have done. He will guide your every step, and He will give you the words to speak. Your assignment in this life does not depend upon your own strength. It depends on hearing His voice and releasing exactly what He has said. Go forth, believing that you are enough, and because He has chosen you, He will fulfill through you all that He has declared.

5

Intimacy

"Hear, O Israel, The Lord our God is one Lord, and thou shalt love the Lord thy God with all thine heart, and with all thy soul, and with all thy might."
Deuteronomy 6:4-5

It's all about Him!

Every breath—every heartbeat—every test—and every struggle isn't about us.

It isn't about our needs, nor about our desires. Not about our lack of strength. It's not even about our healing.

Spending time with Him is just simply that—time alone with Him! It's not about anyone or anything else.

He already knows you. He knew you before you were ever thought about.

He knows every need and every concern. He's seen every wound and every shortcoming.

The magnificent part is He's already declared your healing and your complete transformation.

Yes, you should discuss these things openly with Him and hear what He has to say about them, but your goal in coming to Him shouldn't be for a solution if you are to pursue intimacy with Him.

If you approach your relationship with Him from a posture of what you need from Him, you'll forever find yourself dissatis-fied and troubled. This is simply because there will always be something you need. But if your posture in approaching Him is just to be with Him and to know Him more, then your love, worship, and adoration is poured out.

When those things are what you bring to offer Him, He shows up, and you will never leave feeling empty or dissatisfied. If you focus your time alone with Him on Him alone, then the byproduct of those encounters is that you become more like Him, and everything else becomes subject to His reign and His goodness.

Intimacy is built sitting alone with Him and asking about **His desires**. It's about finding out what **His thoughts** are over every situation you're presented with.

It's about asking Him how you can be a part of His plan and expanding His Kingdom.

True revelation of His fullness begins and ends in your time with Him.

Search

I search for Him, to know Him, to become like Him.
I search for Him to release Him into the world around me.
So, in troubles, in chaos, in distress,
When my heart is overwhelmed and hurting,
I run to Him!
Just to experience Him again…
Just to hear His voice…
Just to feel Him near…
For in those moments…
Everything is okay!

6

Sovereignty

"... all things were created by Him and for Him."
Colossians 1:16

Would you dare allow someone to convince you He is not good? He alone is King and He alone is Sovereign. Furthermore, He reigns from the place of His goodness.

His goodness will always look like His purpose being fulfilled—because He is God and knows all things well. He knows the best way to bring about His purpose.

He's not a toxic or narcissistic God, but His goodness doesn't mean He's a free bubblegum machine where every flavor is your favorite either.

It does mean His goodness is governed by His Sovereignty, and the outcome will always be for your good—not your choice—nor what you think would be easiest or best—But **for your good!**

7

Trust

"Take my yoke upon you, and learn of me; for I am meek and lowly in heart: and ye shall find rest unto your souls." Matthew 11:29-30

Sometimes, life can get the best of us and taint our view of everything around us... if we allow it. Trust is absolutely necessary to experience the peace He has promised us.

Trusting Him means you can lay back in His arms knowing all things are handled by the King of the entire universe. He's got it all figured out. Your circumstance never caught Him off guard. Your fall didn't blindside Him either.

Your trust in Him will be secure in the belief that whatever He chooses to bring out of your current situation is going to be exactly what is best for you.

Trust will say, *"Father, I don't need to know the outcome right now. I don't need to know when or how you will do it. I don't need to know what it will look like in the process. I don't need the answer. I just want to be with You! My trust knows You are perfect and am certain You have all things under control... I just want to be with You!"*

Your trust in an incredible Father will cause you to find a rest that will replace the uncertainty that has surrounded you for far too long.

Stay Awhile

Don't rush away, there are things that I want to say.
I want to breathe new life into the chaos in your mind.
I want to heal the hurt and make new what you have tried so hard to hide.
Stay awhile. Drink of Me.
Stay awhile. Lean into Me.
Stay awhile.
I've waited for you to find this place.
Now, stay awhile and rest in Me.
Here, alone with Me,
Strength is renewed,
Hope is restored,
Every fear will subside as your path becomes clear.
It's all okay, right here at this moment—alone with Me.

8

It's All For Him

"But you are a chosen race, a royal priesthood, a holy nation, a people for His own possession, that you may proclaim the excellencies of Him who called you out of darkness into His marvelous light." 1 Peter 2:9 ESV

Everything pertaining to you and affecting you is His concern—it's His responsibility. It is His absolute pleasure to take care of them. Dying to self declares loudly—IT'S ALL HIS!

Your responsibility in this life is Him. It is hearing Him and acting out His will and His instructions. Therein is where His life, being lived out through you, is profoundly increased. Your life and desires are laid down at His feet. The life you now live is by faith in Christ Jesus.

Believe in Him; therefore, give Him all of your being to do as He wishes. Your purpose is to release Him throughout the earth in every situation you are placed in.

This is the purpose of fasting: to subdue your flesh so that what you hear above everything is His voice and not your own desires. Your flesh is silenced by fasting so you can hear Him speak with more clarity.

It's crucial that we become a people who hear His voice over every situation we are placed in. What He is speaking will come to pass when we believe and live out His word.

9

His Kingdom

**"...and of His Kingdom there shall be no end."
Luke 1:32-33**

Sometimes our human nature can get caught up in the work we are called to do and allow it to become our identity. We look for an end goal to be the place of His Kingdom work.

To explain further, we start to think when we reach THIS certain place, when we are doing THIS certain work, when we have attained THIS certain position, or we are performing THIS certain duty in His Kingdom... then we have arrived. But I tell you, His Kingdom work never ends.

Establishing His Kingdom within you is a day-by-day and moment-by-moment journey. Only then will there be a release through you. It isn't a location you eventually get to. It is established each day in every circumstance. It is released by imitating Him. It is established by living like Him. Heaven on Earth is something you build, something you partner with God to see come to fruition in every place you enter and to every person you encounter.

It is a continual thing to release His Kingdom. It's a continual establishing through hearing what His desire is over things and people surrounding us. It is getting into His Presence, hearing His desire and instructions for a specific situation, and carrying them out as He leads. It's a partnership, and it doesn't end.

Silence The Noise

Though everything around you has gotten noisy,
Though everything around you bids for your attention, Even though distractions are a constant complication,
All He wants you to focus on is Him.
Be alone with Him.
Hear His voice.
Be alone with Him.
Hear His voice.
Be alone with Him.
Hear His voice.
Steal away to be with Him.
Hear His voice.
Run to Him—just to be with Him.
Hear His voice.
Sit in silence if you must—just to be with Him.
And above all, wait…
To hear His voice.

10

Battling Uncertainty

"For my thoughts are not your thoughts, neither are your ways my ways, saith the Lord." Isaiah 55:8

Uncertainty is when you cannot lay out what is going to happen in your current situation. It can come upon you quickly, especially when your plan looks nothing like the path you followed. Uncertainty is when someone else has control of a situation concerning you and the details aren't made known to you.

Certainty, on the other hand, is a beautiful level of trust in who has control of the situation. Trusting they are more than capable of handling every detail, and your connection to them will mean the outcome will be in your favor.

You can face these things when your life seems to be in a season of pause. You can find yourself dwelling on the uncertainty of the situation and becoming unsure of everything.

"What am I feeling?

"Why did I feel that way?

"What is going on?

"What should I do?'
"Is this the right decision?
"Did I hear Him right, or did I miss the mark on this?
"This hurts; I don't know if I actually heard Him correctly."

In these circumstances, you can find yourself wanting to talk things out with someone, where you desperately want someone to give you confirmation that you are on the right path.

Instead, He is standing beside you, gently calling you closer to Him.

And He says, with the comfort only a Father can provide in the chaos:

> *Will you just talk with Me about it? Will you pour it all out to Me and ask Me what I am thinking?"*

11

Acknowledge

"In all your ways acknowledge Him, and He shall direct your paths." Proverbs 3:5-6

Before you were ever formed in your mother's womb, He spoke over you a divine purpose to fulfill in His Kingdom. Although His words are creative and definite, He has allowed your free will to be the deciding factor in how much of this purpose you fulfill. Your "yes" to Him allows you to partner with Him to fulfill what was spoken over you from the beginning of time.

His promise to you cannot be altered or changed by anything but your inability to say yes and believe. You must see this from the lens of His goodness and trust that He is for us. You will never be able to believe if you are just hoping He will be good to you and take care of you. He takes great pleasure in providing for you as you seek Him and His desires.

He is asking you as His child to simply acknowledge that He is your God. He is sovereign and King over all. He also wants you to acknowledge that His hand is upon you and He has chosen you for such a time as this. Your acknowledgment is your admission and agreement with Him that He has a divinely inspired plan for your life. When you confess that His hand is upon you and He has chosen you, your entire being begins to respond to the words He has spoken over you.

It is your spoken faith that gives Him the "yes" He desires to hear. It is your spoken confession that causes you to express in faith that His words are true, and He will perform all He says He will perform. Allow yourself the honor to sit alone with Him and verbally acknowledge that He has a purpose for your life. Ask Him to show you this purpose and to give you the grace and strength to walk into it.

- Father, I acknowledge Your goodness over my life.
- I acknowledge Your favor over my life.
- I acknowledge Your words over me, and I agree those words are life.
- I acknowledge You have chosen me, and I choose to partner with You to see those things fulfilled.
- Lead me step by step, Father, that my life will bring You glory.

His Great Love: My Story

I acknowledge His love for me is great.
The things He has granted unto me are far more than I deserve. The places He will take me in relationship with Him, I did not earn.
I walked away from Him. I ran in the opposite direction, attempting to flee the trauma I refused to heal from.
I chose filth and shame and turned my back on Him.
I chose chaos and self-destruction over His love. cut myself continually in the graveyards of my past, trying to find closure and identity.
But, He drew me when I wasn't walking towards or even searching for Him.
HE CAME TO ME!
He found me in the midst of all the dry bones that signified the destruction I had allowed to be.
Then, in the place of my destruction, He commanded me to live.
He picked me up from the ashes, carried me into His chamber, and spoke words of love over me.
He whispered who I was into the deepest recesses of my soul.
He kissed my brow and wiped away the confusion.
He breathed deep into me the existence of who He was calling me to be.
He held me against His chest until I could see and acknowledge His great love for me.
As He embraced me, I realized…
I had fallen in love with Him.
I am His… and He is mine.

12

Change Your Mindset

"Do not let yourself be overcome by evil, but overcome evil with good." Romans 12:21

This scripture has long been my call to change the way I view my journey to becoming all that God has called me to be. In our quest to be like Him, we can become so focused on what we need to change that we forget to focus our mind on what is important. As long as we are alive, our human nature (our flesh) will pull us toward selfish motives. Our attention should be more focused on doing what is good rather than the opposite.

I know this sounds completely contradictory to everything you have been taught to believe. However, the Word of God does not lie. As you begin this new journey of healing and wholeness, you may be overwhelmed with the changes required to be more like Him. But do not be weary in doing well.

This does not mean that you ignore the areas in your lives which do not align with the Will and Word of God. However, you must be cautious not to develop a mindset that only nurtures what is negative or requires change. This can overshadow the good within you that overcomes evil.

As you embark on this amazing journey of healing that God has laid before you, focus daily on intentionally doing what is right according to the Word.

Here are practical ways to adjust and mature spiritually:

1. **Be intentional about seeking God by reading the Bible.** He is the Word; therefore, the Word is life. It teaches you how to live correctly, and when you indulge in the words of God Himself, it breathes life into the new beginning you are launching into.
2. **Spend time in His Presence.** Turn on worship music, listen to the Word audibly. Whatever it takes to turn your mind and your affections toward Him, do it! Allow yourself to spend time in His Presence talking about the things that press on you and how you feel about them. It is moments in His Presence that wash and regenerate you to become more and more like Him (Titus 3:5).
3. **Be vigilant about keeping your thoughts and actions toward Him.** You were designed to bring Him glory. So all that you do and say can be a constant flow of things that glorify Him and cause others to want to know Him personally. Keeping your mind upon Him will bring you into a place of perfect peace according to Isaiah 26:3: *"Thou will keep him in perfect peace, whose mind is stayed on thee: because he trusteth in thee."*

As you go forward in this new life, living from a place of healing and wholeness, you will learn what it is like to live in peace. Learning to live in such a place is just as important as allowing yourself to heal.

Approach every situation with grace. Allow yourself space to adjust so you can operate in that moment as a healed person. Going forward, carry the mindset of being made new.

Milton Keynes UK
Ingram Content Group UK Ltd.
UKHW020819141124
451149UK00020B/1127